PUT YOUR SH*T AWAY!

A BEDTIME STORY FOR THE MESSY

BY KIM DALLARA

ILLUSTRATIONS BY ALEXANDRA RUSU

Printed in the United States of America

ISBN 978-1-953910-17-2 (hardcover)
ISBN 978-1-953910-16-5 (paperback)

Canoe Tree Press
4697 Main Street
Manchester Center, VT 05255

Canoe Tree Press is a division of DartFrog Books.

FOR MY HUSBAND:
MY LOVE AND INSPIRATION.

HI, LOVE.
BEFORE YOU TURN OFF THE LIGHT,
I HAVE A FAVOR TO ASK...

Please

put your
sh*t away!

LOOK AT THOSE **FIVE**
HALF-FULL CUPS OF WATER
ON THE NIGHTSTAND.

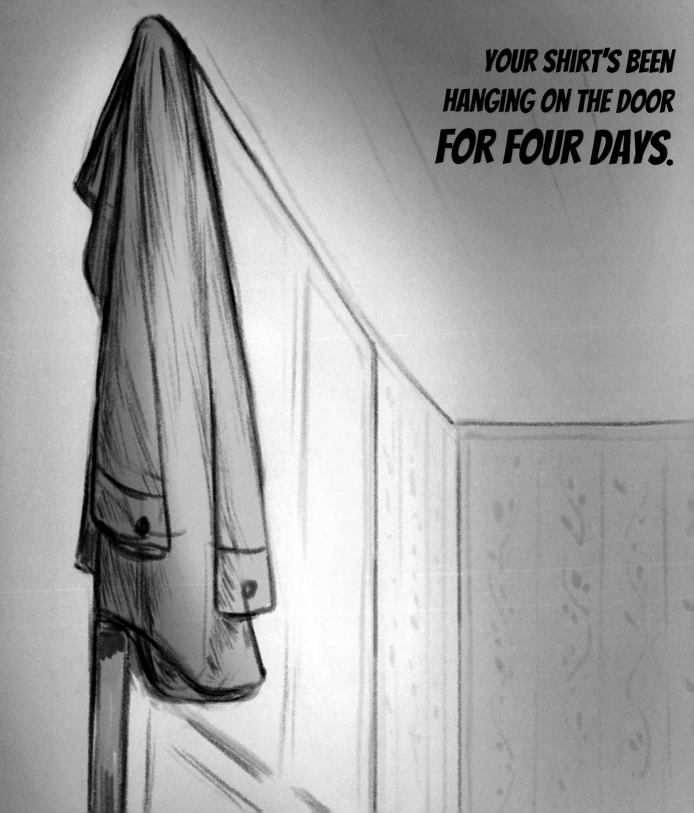

YOUR SHIRT'S BEEN HANGING ON THE DOOR **FOR FOUR DAYS.**

10

THAT PILE OF RECEIPTS WILL NOT EVER BE USEFUL. **EVER.**

WE HAVE **$318**
IN BEER-MAKING SUPPLIES
TO SAVE **$.05** PER PINT

THERE'S A MASSIVE TANGLE OF
ELECTRICAL CORDS
IN THE LAUNDRY ROOM THAT
DON'T GO
WITH ANYTHING WE OWN.

AND THE FLOPPY DISCS.
AN ENTIRE BOX OF
FLOPPY DISCS?

15

DO YOU KNOW HOW A TOWEL BAR WORKS?

AND THE USED BANDAGE ON THE COUNTER,
WELL THAT'S JUST F*CKING GROSS.

Your

sh*t is
Everywhere!

WHAT'S THAT YOU SAY?
WE MIGHT NEED IT SOMEDAY?
NO. NO WE WON'T.

ALL THIS SH*T CAN GO
TO THE MAGICAL LAND OF AWAY.

THAT'S ALL!
SLEEP TIGHT.
I LOVE YOU.

ABOUT THE AUTHOR

Kim Dallara is an author of average skill and above-average sarcasm. A self-professed neat freak, she lives with her husband in a home that seems to be shrinking in size by the day. This is her first book, and a Hail Mary effort at encouraging her husband to finally put away his sh*t.

Made in the USA
Middletown, DE
10 December 2020

26974281R00018